SCIENTIFIC AMERICAN | EDUCATIONAL PUBLISHING

SCIENTIFIC AMERICAN INVESTIGATES FOSSILS

PLANT FOSSILS

BY NATALIE HUMPHREY

Published in 2025 by The Rosen Publishing Group
in association with Scientific American Educational Publishing
2544 Clinton Street, Buffalo NY 14224

Cataloging-in-Publication Data
Names: Humphrey, Natalie.
Title: Plant fossils / Natalie Humphrey.
Description: New York : Scientific American Educational Publishing, an imprint of Rosen Publishing, 2025. | Series: Scientific American investigates fossils | Includes glossary and index.
Identifiers: ISBN 9781725352070 (pbk.) | ISBN 9781725352087 (library bound) | ISBN 9781725352094 (ebook)
Subjects: LCSH: Plants, Fossil–Juvenile literature.
Classification: LCC QE906.H86 2025 | DDC 561–dc23

Portions of this work were originally authored by Kathleen Connors and published as *Plant Fossils*. All new material in this edition is authored by Natalie Humphrey.

Designer: Andrea Davison-Bartolotta
Editor: Natalie Humphrey

Photo credits: Cover, p. 1 (main) servickuz/Shutterstock.com; cover, p. 1 (vingette) Yurlick/Shutterstock.com; p. 5 Robert Schneider/Shutterstock.com; p. 7 Geraint Duval/Shutterstock.com; p. 9 Nuntiya/Shutterstock.com; pp. 11, 15 James St. John/Flickr.com; p. 13 Alla chesnokova/iStockphoto.com; p. 15 BlueBarronPhoto/Shutterstock.com; p. 17 NPGallery/NPS.gov; p. 19 Wilson44691/File:Viburnum lesquereuxii fossil.jpg; p. 20 alice-photo/Shutterstock.com; p. 21 Michelle Waycott/File:Seagrass Evolution.svg.

Printed in the United States of America

CPSIA compliance information: Batch #CWSA25. For Further Information contact Rosen Publishing at 1-800-237-9932.

CONTENTS

Words in the glossary appear in **bold** type the first time they are used in the text.

FOSSILIZED PLANTS

To understand what the ancient world may have looked like, scientists study plant fossils! Through these fossils, scientists can learn what Earth's **climate** might have been like. They can even tell if a certain place used to be **underwater**.

While plant fossils can be found around the world, they aren't as common as animal fossils. But when scientists can find these fossils, it can help to create a clearer idea of what our planet looked like millions of years ago.

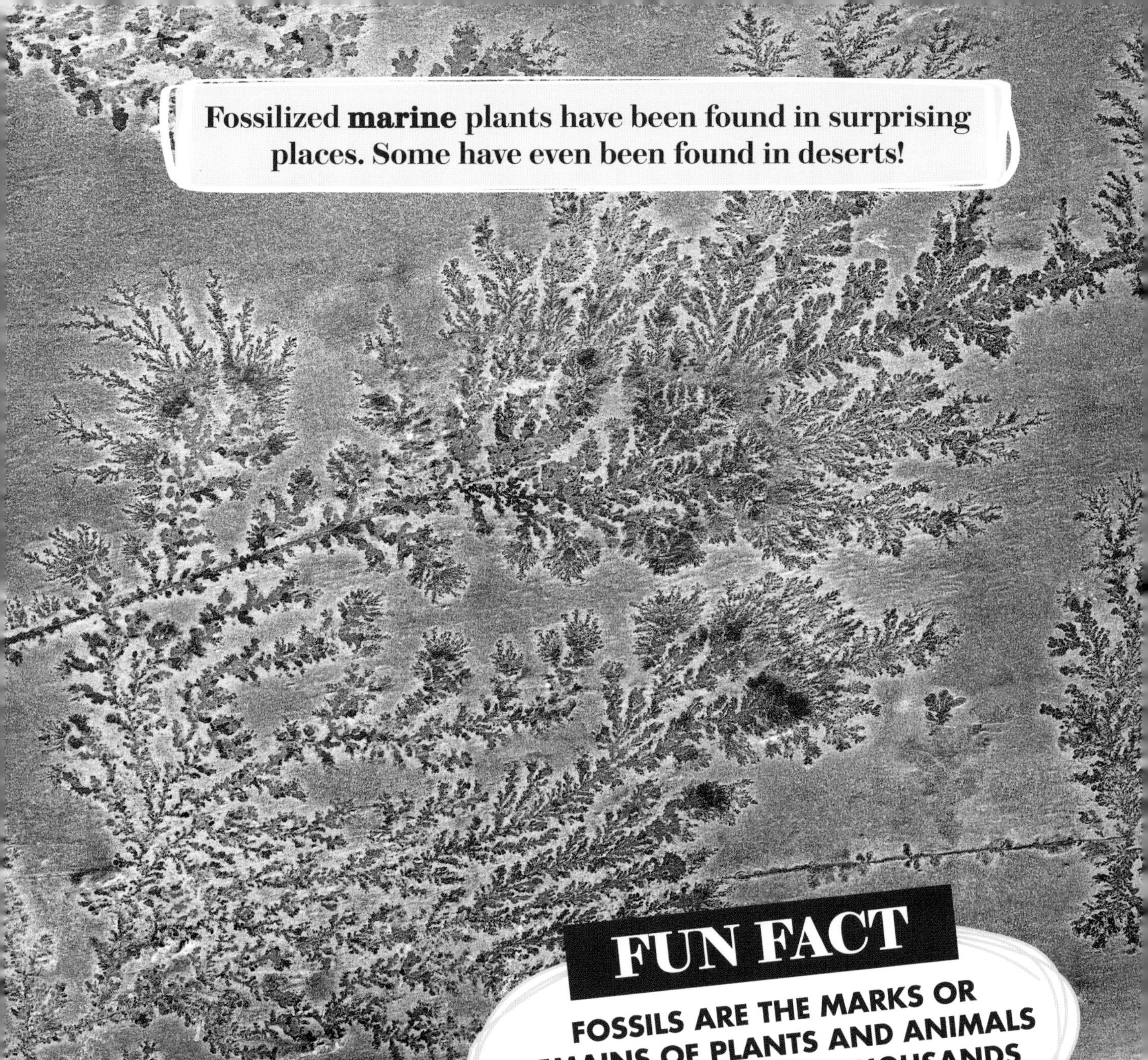

Fossilized **marine** plants have been found in surprising places. Some have even been found in deserts!

FUN FACT

FOSSILS ARE THE MARKS OR REMAINS OF PLANTS AND ANIMALS THAT FORMED OVER THOUSANDS OR MILLIONS OF YEARS.

PALEOBOTANISTS

A paleobotanist is a person who studies plant fossils. "Paleo" means ancient. "Botany" is the study of plants. A paleobotanist often studies one special kind of plant fossil, such as flowers or trees.

One part of paleobotany is palynology, or the study of spores and pollen. Scientists have studied many of these tiny plant parts because they have been well **preserved** over time. Scientists learn about the weather in an area by looking at spore and pollen fossils.

Some fossilized plant spores are up to 480 million years old. This image shows a fossilized plant spore up close.

FUN FACT

SPORES ARE SMALL BODIES MADE BY A PLANT THAT CAN GROW INTO ANOTHER PLANT. MANY PLANTS TODAY, SUCH AS FERNS AND MOSSES, STILL SPREAD USING SPORES.

DELICATE FOSSILS

Plant fossils can be hard to find. This is because many plant parts are too delicate, or easily torn or harmed, to become fossils. Some common plant fossils are pollen, spores, and woody plants that don't break down easily. Scientists have found fruit and seed fossils too. Fossilized flowers, however, are harder to find.

Plant fossils form when plants or plant parts are buried in **sediment**. Over thousands or millions of years, the sediment turns to rock and preserves the plant inside.

It may take a long time for scientists to figure out what kind of plant a fossil is from.

FUN FACT

PLANTS ARE OFTEN FOSSILIZED NEAR BODIES OF WATER WITH A LOT OF MOVING SEDIMENT SUCH AS LAKES, AND RIVERS.

MORE PLANT FOSSILS

Compression fossils form under **pressure**. The pressure compresses, or flattens, the plant parts and changes the sediment around the plant into rock. Compression fossils may also preserve the organic, or living, matter.

Impressions are prints of a plant. Sometimes, the same plant creates both a compression and an impression. When a rock is split apart, the fossilized remains of the plant matter stick to one side of it. This side is the compression. The other side is often a print of the plant, or the impression.

Does this impression remind you of any plant you know?

COMPRESSION FOSSIL

IMPRESSION FOSSIL

FUN FACT

IN FOSSILS THAT HAVE BOTH A COMPRESSION AND AN IMPRESSION, THE COMPRESSION IS CALLED THE PART. THE IMPRESSION IS CALLED THE COUNTERPART.

PERMINERALIZATION

Sometimes, a plant fossil forms through permineralization (puhr-mih-nuh-ruhl-ih-ZAY-shun). Permineralization occurs when **minerals** and water flow into a plant buried in sediment. These minerals fill the empty spaces and small holes in the plants.

Plants can create cast and mold fossils as well. After being buried in sediment, plant matter often breaks down, leaving behind a space in the shape of the plant. This is called a mold. When the mold fills with sediment, a fossil called a cast is formed.

Petrified wood is a common type of petrified plant fossil.

FUN FACT

IF MINERALS TAKE THE PLACE OF ALL THE PLANT'S PARTS, THIS IS CALLED A PETRIFIED FOSSIL.

PLANT EVOLUTION

Plants evolve, or change over time! Plant fossils help paleontologists put together a timeline of plant evolution. They've learned plants didn't live on land until about 470 to 500 million years ago. The first forests appeared about 390 million years ago. Scientists think the earliest fossils of plants known as angiosperms date back 100 to 145 million years.

Scientists believe plants started as tiny marine plants called phytoplankton. These phytoplankton are known today as green **algae**.

Scientists believe the first phytoplankton may have been on the Earth as early as 3 billion years ago.

FUN FACT

ANGIOSPERMS ARE PLANTS THAT GROW THEIR SEEDS INSIDE FLOWERS OR FRUIT. GYMNOSPERMS, SUCH AS EVERGREEN TREES, GROW SEEDS INSIDE CONES.

FLOWERING PLANTS

Angiosperms today are usually called "flowering plants." But the earliest angiosperm fossils don't show plants with flowers. These plants probably looked more like small bushes. Some flower fossils date back as far as 174 million years. Plants with big, showy flowers started to grow in large numbers about 95 million years ago.

Fossilized flowers aren't common. **Petals** break down too easily to be preserved. Paleobotanists have to study fossilized fruits, seeds, and pollen to learn what these plants were like.

Today, there are over 300,000 species, or kinds, of flowering plants.

PLANTS AND INSECTS

When scientists find a plant fossil, they often find an **insect** fossil nearby. This is because insects and plants evolved together. Early plants needed help pollinating. They grew flowers to draw animals to them. Insects fed from the flowers. They even grew special mouthparts to do so!

Plant fossils help scientists learn about the places ancient animals lived. By studying plant fossils found near dinosaur fossils, paleontologists can figure out whether the dinosaur lived in forests or dry grasslands.

Some plant fossils, such as this one, show marks from where they were eaten by insects.

FINDING PLANT FOSSILS

Plant fossils can be hard to find, but you can still see them! One of the best places to see plant fossils is a **museum**. The Field Museum in Chicago, Illinois, is a great place to see plant fossils. You can also see plant fossils at the New York State Museum.

Some plant fossils can also be found in national parks. At Petrified Forest National Park in Arizona, visitors can see many tree fossils.

Timeline of Plant Evolution

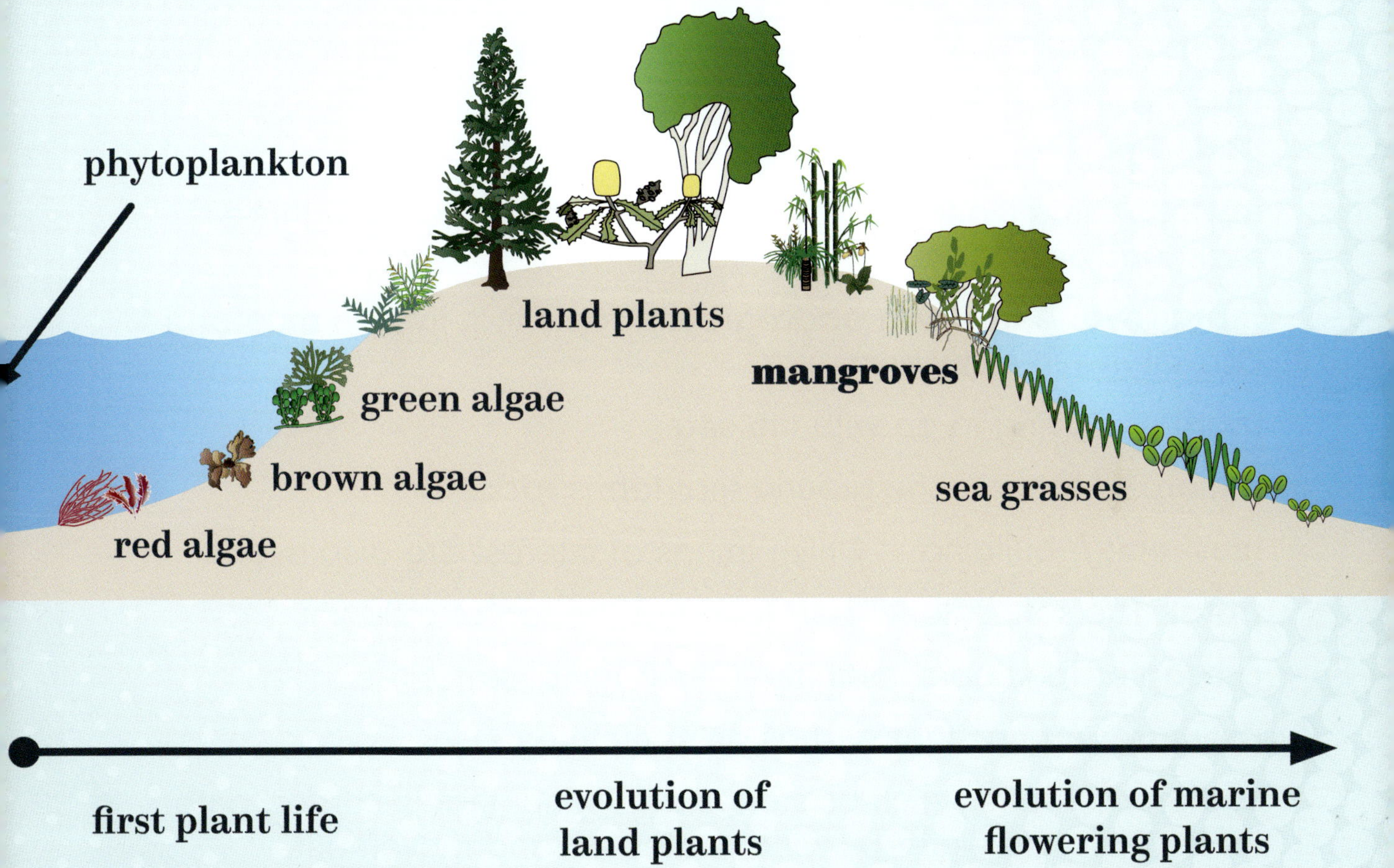

GLOSSARY

algae: Plantlike living things that are mostly found in water.

climate: The average weather conditions of a place over a period of time.

insect: A small, often winged, animal with six legs and three main body parts.

mangrove: A tree with aboveground roots that lives in mud and can survive in saltwater.

marine: Having to do with the sea.

mineral: Matter in the ground that forms rocks.

museum: A building in which things of interest are displayed.

petal: The soft, colorful part found at the top of a flower.

preserve: To keep something in its original state.

pressure: A force that pushes on something else.

sediment: Matter, such as stones and sand, that is carried onto land or into the water by wind, water, or land movement.

underwater: Beneath the top layer of the water.

FOR MORE INFORMATION

Books

Hibbert, Claire. *Plants*. Buffalo, NY: Gareth Stevens Publishing, 2023.

Hicks, Kelli L. *Fossils and Ancient Plants*. New York, NY: Crabtree Publishing Company, 2022.

Websites

Britannica Kids: Fossils
https://kids.britannica.com/kids/article/fossil/353144
Learn more about how different fossils form and where they are found.

Natural History Museum: Prehistoric Plants
www.nhm.ac.uk/discover/how-to-grow-a-dinosaur-garden.html
Discover different prehistoric plants and learn how to grow your own dinosaur garden.

Publisher's note to educators and parents: Our editors have carefully reviewed these websites to ensure that they are suitable for students. Many websites change frequently, however, and we cannot guarantee that a site's future contents will continue to meet our high standards of quality and educational value. Be advised that students should be closely supervised whenever they access the internet.

INDEX